Getting Business for Your Business

Do-It-Yourself Strategies to Increase Your Small Business' Bottom Line

By L.A. Dyer

Copyright © 2018 L.A. Dyer

All rights reserved. No part of this book may be reproduced in any form or by any electronic or mechanical means, including information storage and retrieval systems, without permission in writing from the publisher and author, except by reviewers, who may quote brief passages in a review.

Cover design by L.A. Dyer

Visit http://www.LADyerbooks.com for more exciting products from this author.

ISBN: 9781729411964

DEDICATION

Special thanks to KDD, MJD, MAD, JLW-B, CB, TB, KB, SER, Shelly the Wonder Dog, and the rest of my family and friends who didn't laugh out loud (in front of me) when I told them what I was doing.

And JJW who said that writing was what was next for me.

To all the courageous entrepreneurs out there, don't let anything stop you. Ever.

CONTENTS

	Acknowledgments	i
1	Getting to What's Next	9
2	Develop Business for Your Business	12
3	Your Promotional Plan	16
4	Marketing, Sales, and Business Development	24
5	The Customer-Centered Business Development Approach	28
6	Build Your Messaging	32
7	Building Your Brand with Marketing Communications	37
8	Tradeshow Strategies	60
9	Social Media	70
10	Your CRM – The Personal Assistant That You Really Need	80
11	Now Go Forth and Make Money	86
	Appendix A: SBA Business Resources	88
	Appendix B: Business Development Overview: Promotional Strategy Based Around a Product	90

ACKNOWLEDGMENTS

Special thanks to Sam E. Rosenhaus for his excellent editing skills, Judith Braley for our weekly meetings, and Kevin Dyer for his excellent perspectives on business.

CHAPTER 1

Getting to What's Next

"It had long since come to my attention that people of accomplishment rarely sat back and let things happen to them. They went out and happened to things." ...*Leonardo da Vinci (1452-1519)*

Starting your own business is a daunting task! After you decide the details of your business, define your processes and policies, register with the government, and set up shop, it may be hard to think about what's next.

This book will help you set up a promotional plan that details and tracks your promotional activities associated with your business. It explains common marketing practices like messaging, marketing communications such as websites, email marketing and brochures, effectively using social media, and setting up a customer relationship management tool to build your customer base. It's a how-to for launching your business into promotion mode and helping you with the "what's next" part of your business journey.

In it I'll show you:

- How to get your ideas into a plan so you have a roadmap to develop business for your business.
- I'll give you an explanation on how marketing and sales strategy both contribute to business development.
- How to develop your message and brand.
- How to choose a tradeshow and get the most customers from it.
- How to craft many of the parts of your promotional strategy yourself, saving you time and money.

Why did I write this book? I have been involved in some facet of business for over 30 years. First, working in civil engineering firms, then with Bell Labs, and moving on to various startups and Fortune 500 companies. I have strategized for a number of different industries including telecom, construction, government, tax, senior care, and software. I have an MBA in marketing and a BFA in graphic design and have held the title of graphic designer, marketing communications strategist, and most recently business development manager. I have created numerous successful branding vehicles, including websites, brochures, business cards, and email newsletters. I have read countless books on advertising, marketing, social media strategy, promotion, and business development. And now, I want to help you get business for your business by explaining how you can get it done for less money than you think.

Do you have an idea for a small business but haven't gotten your ideas down on paper? In the back of this book I've included some resources from the Small Business Administration (SBA.GOV) to assist you with getting started.

There is a workbook that accompanies this book named *The Getting Business for Your Business Workbook*. It's a personal business diary for you to write down all of your ideas, goals, thoughts, and create a plan for your dream business.

Thank you for purchasing and reading my book. It was a joy to write knowing that I could help you cash in with my knowledge. And if you like my book, please leave me a favorable review on Amazon, because like you, I'm trying to develop business for my business. And thank you in advance for doing that.

Now go forth and make money!

CHAPTER 2

Develop Business for Your Business

Developing business for your business. As an entrepreneur, it's the one thing I think about the most. What if no one buys what I'm selling? How will I get the word out that I've got the most amazing product or service (or eBook) available to the entire world? It all starts with a promotional plan and then action.

Business development in the traditional sense is about developing long-term relationships that result in increased brand awareness and sales for your business. It combines all your digital and traditional marketing, product/service strategy, communications/messaging, customer service strategy, sales strategy, tradeshow strategy, and competitor strategy (along with others) to enhance and build your relationships with customers. And then turn those customers into friends who eventually (and organically) morph into partners who are long term. Finding customers who will market your business for you for free because they like your product or service (or you!) so much is priceless. You can do this by providing a better way to pay, a better website experience or a better customer experience. All these things develop your business and make you better at it – which makes it better for your customer. Which is honestly what we all want.

Developing business for your business starts with you, the business owner. YOU are the biggest cheerleader for your product or service. Because you know what? Your enthusiasm is contagious! And your enthusiasm for your P/S (from now on in this book I will use P/S to stand for 'product or service') translates to enthusiasm for your customer. Because a happy and satisfied customer is your ultimate goal as they are more apt to SHARE that enthusiasm with strangers that will become customers, friends, and partners. And that increases your profit. CH-CHING! I can hear your cash rolling in right now!

To me, business development is an art and a science – there's no perfect way to do it. It completely depends on your P/S and it depends on you as a business owner.

Here are some simple truths that I believe:

- The customer is always right. A happy, satisfied customer should be a your goal.

- Always try your best to manage expectations (of your customers, employees and your suppliers). Don't promise things you can't deliver!
- Excitement and confidence about your P/S translates to excitement for your customers and employees.
- Happy, enthusiastic, knowledgeable employees help make happy customers.
- **GRIT** is the thing you need to run a small business. Opening and sustaining a small business is truly the hardest thing you will most likely ever do besides, maybe, parenting a child. But it's worth it. There will be times when you want to say "No more. I'm quitting!" But don't! Just keep going. You're going to hit a wall, you know. It's where you think you can't do it and you hang it up and don't look back. But think about the end – what you want to happen and how successful you want to be and how you'll feel great working for yourself – and keep going. You'll get there. It takes time, but with dedication and perseverance it will happen.

Just an FYI, Thomas Edison failed over a thousand times before inventing the light bulb. So if that's not grit, I don't know what is.

WRITE IT DOWN:

Did you know that Thomas Edison also took a day every few weeks to just sit and think about his inventions/business? Give yourself the freedom to do the same thing because your ideas about your business are important! Sit and think about your business, P/S, customers, and employees. Why not sit in a coffee shop/home/outside under a tree/on a bench while your kids are busy at the playground/the beach/park/kitchen table/doing their chores and think out your business plan? If you purchased my workbook *The Getting Business for Your Business Workbook*, please turn to Chapter 2 to get your business ideas and goals down on paper.

CHAPTER 3

Your Promotional Plan

Your promotional plan is an outline for your business. It describes how you are going to get customers, keep customers, and develop customers into partners.

<u>DO NOT AVOID DOING A PLAN!</u>

Your promotional plan is part of your business plan. Your promotional plan is a way to implement the goals, strategy, tactics, and objectives for going to market that you have outlined in your business plan. Pardon the marketing gobbledygook there, but it had to be done.

A quick, simple, and dirty tutorial on marketing strategy:

- **Goals:** How much of your P/S do you want to sell? How many customers do you want to have? What's your dream monthly revenue? These will be some of your goals. You will accomplish them by describing your objectives, outlining your strategies, and implementing your tactics (actions).
- **Marketing objectives:** A marketing objective is a long-term marketing goal. It's really your marketing "Target". Examples would be:
  - To increase revenue
  - To increase brand awareness
- **Strategy:** This is your plan of action. How are you going to reach your objectives? Are you using a low pricing strategy? A product differentiation strategy? A technological strategy? Once you figure out your strategy, then you move on to your tactics.
- **Tactics:** Tactics are the activities that you will perform to implement your strategies to reach your objectives. They are the "how". So with the strategies described above, your tactics would be:
  - Low price tactic: When you go to market, you will price your product lower than your competitors leading to their decreased market share and your increased market share. Because of your lower price, you will need to sell more to make an even profit.

- Product differentiation tactic: how is your P/S different from your competitors? In your marketing and sales strategy, you must stress the positive differences of your P/S.
- A technological tactic: Will you use texting, mobile apps, or have any technological advantage over your competitor?

WRITE IT DOWN: Did you know that you are more apt to accomplish you goals if you write them down? Yes. It is a proven truth. And when you write down the goal, list three things that you will do to accomplish that goal. And if you really want to knock it out of the park - add some dates! In chapter 2 of my workbook, there is a section for recording your business goals and accompanying activities.

Before you begin, develop your elevator pitch. If you were going to persuade an investor to invest in your company/P/S and you only had one minute to do it, how would you describe your offering to persuade someone to give you money? When writing, pretend you are charging yourself $100 per word and write out a one minute pitch like you were in an elevator with an investor or a customer. Pitch it to friends and family and see if they would invest!

Strengths, weaknesses, opportunities, and threats (SWOT). Taken from traditional marketing, the SWOT analysis is a critical tool in evaluating your competitors and your ability to thrive in the market that your want to target. The strengths and weaknesses are things that are internal to your business. Examples of strengths would be your new products or services, a new customer experience, or a new website design. Weaknesses would be improvements you could make or an internal problem that cost you sales (bad employees, machine breakdowns). Opportunities and threats are external to your business. Examples of opportunities would be a good economy or new trends that allow for new products. And examples of threats would be new products from competitors or changing technological issues that you haven't implemented.

- What is the current economy? Good/bad?
- What is the current state of your industry?
- Are there any trends that you could use to increase sales?
- What are the strengths of your P/S/you?
- What are the weaknesses of your P/S/you?
- What opportunities do you see in the future?
- What threats do you see in the future?
- What is your pricing strategy?
    - When you think about this, do you have a different price points? For example, do you have differentiated level of pricing like a luxury line?

Competitors. Your competitors can be a great source of inspiration. Remember, your competitors are going to directly target YOUR customers so it's good to know as much as you can about them. Set up an area of your plan dedicated to competitors.

- How do you think your P/S is different from your competitors?
- Why should people purchase from you?
- What is the present situation of the environment that you are entering?
- How many competitors are there?
- How long have they been in the industry?
- How much money do they make?
- How many customers do they have?
- What's their differentiator?
- What is the pricing strategy of your competitors?

Ideas to implement right now! Read the reviews of your competitors. Focus on the bad ones and make sure you DON'T do these things. Bad reviews represent a great opportunity for you!

Check your local library! Many public libraries have excellent business research resources. I prefer to research competitors on Hoovers Online and Mergent. It's great for customer or competitor research and includes sample business plans! Check your local library for details.

Also, have you heard of S.C.O.R.E.? As the website states: SCORE is the nation's largest network of volunteer, expert business mentors, with more than 10,000 volunteers in 300 chapters.

As a resource partner of the U.S. Small Business Administration (SBA), SCORE has helped more than 10 million entrepreneurs through mentoring, workshops and educational resources since 1964.

SCORE has helped many first-time entrepreneurs navigate the process of opening and sustaining a business. You can see more of their free services at score.org.

Your unique customer experience. How do you see your customers reacting to your product? Excited? Inquisitive? This helps with your customer experience. Whether it's a point & click or it's someone coming into your store, or someone using your service by just speaking with you over phone, I would suggest thinking out the experience you would like the customer to have. This helps when you are planning and running your business. Besides, these days, remember it's all about the experience!

Other questions to answer in your plan that you will help you:

- What CRM (Customer Relationship Management) software will you use?
- Who will set it up?
- Who will use it? How many users will you have?

- What new markets can you think of? This is a question you should put on a laminated post-it somewhere you will see it everyday or write them in your business diary.

Your customers want what's original. And guess what? That's you! The perception of your business really boils down to who you are. So bring your thoughts, talents, sense of humor and caring for the customer. What a customer feels about your P/S has a direct impact on your sales, so put your uniqueness all over your business and your sales will benefit. An example: when I did business development for a small tax services company, I put much of my marketing strategy around the owner of the company. Many of his customers knew him and I crafted the marketing message around his honesty and integrity and that resonated with customers. And those customers liked him so much that it was easy for them to recommend his service to other clients (free marketing!). These customers are an excellent example of partners.

Let's think from the end for a moment. Look at where you want your business to be in 6 months, one year, two years, four years, and eight years.

Okay, let's look at your six month plan.

- How much do you want to make?
- If you have a product, who are your suppliers?
- If you have a service, how will you implement it?

- How many customers do you want to have?
- How many long-term relationships will you develop?
- What major expenses will you have? Where are you getting the money to pay them?
- What is your sales strategy? How will you get that business? (Keep reading this book and I will help you with this).
- How will you promote your P/S? Advertising/social media/website/tradeshows/home parties?

Now, do the same thing for one, two, four, and eight years. Keep checking and updating this list and change it as needed. This will help you determine the tactics (activities) you will need to undertake to accomplish your daily, monthly, and yearly goals.

CHAPTER 4

Marketing, Sales, and Business Development

Your marketing efforts will directly affect your sales volume. There are many different types of marketing that provide promotional activities for your business.

- Digital marketing
- Social media marketing
- Traditional marketing
- Customer relationship marketing
- Website marketing
- Email marketing
- Employee marketing
- Tradeshow marketing

- Content marketing

The Four Ps of Marketing

Price: Where is your price in terms of the market and your competition? Are you at the bottom, top, or middle? What price point will the market (your customers) pay with the least amount of resistance? Do you offer coupons, discounts, or promo codes?

Place: Where are you selling? Tradeshow, brick and mortar store, online, through a distribution network, out of your home?

Product: (Your service is also your product) What are the functions of your P/S? What's the packaging? Describe the branding that you think will suit your P/S.

Promotion: How are you going to advertise/promote? All marketing communications would fall under "promotion" like brochures, websites, logos, stationary, and pretty much any messaging that goes out to your customer.

How Do Marketing and Sales Work Together?

Good marketing strengthens sales. When you (or your salesperson) meet with a customer to discuss your P/S, you rely on your marketing research, message, the functionality of your website, the brochure that has been produced, and the P/S itself. Marketing is always working in the background to increase sales.

And in a small business, you are the Marketing Director and

the Sales Director and often, the main salesperson and it's important that you know exactly what to say to persuade your customer to buy. If you did the recommended research that I listed in the previous chapter, when designing your marketing and sales message you will know how to use that information to influence sales. When you speak to your customer (or supplier or investor) you will have the knowledge to grab market share away from your competitor, speak clearly about your P/S and industry, and grab that all important sale. This, in your customer's eyes, puts you in a position of authority and in turn, builds trust in you and your P/S. Gaining the trust of a customer is important, so load yourself up with knowledge!

A great sales/marketing person knows how to listen, too. When your customer provides that all-important feedback, it can strengthen your marketing. Listen to your customers! They'll tell you why they are or aren't buying.

A few words about sales. Let me make the disclaimer that I am not a true salesperson. But I do sell stuff everyday in the form of ideas to my kids, and I have watched some great salespeople in action. Here are some things that I've learned about great sales strategy and salespeople:

- A good salesperson knows their P/S inside and out and can describe, in detail, the benefits of it to the customer.
- Never, ever disparage your competitor. Your customer may have purchased from them in the past and when you

say that your competitor is bad to that customer, you're saying that the customer's choice was wrong and in turn your are disparaging your customer. Instead, take the weakness of your competitor and turn them into strengths for your P/S.

> ➢ An example would be if your competitor has bad customer service. Take that information when speaking with your customer and stress how good your customer service is never even saying the name of your competitor.

- Exude confidence but not arrogance.
- Always keep in mind how you are helping the customer.
- Be honest.
- Be friendly.
- Listen intently.
- Envision your success in the end.
- Always follow up with a call, text, or email – usually within 1-2 hours.
- If you have a service business, always provide a quote. A quote is a great way to be able to get in front of your customer discussing the benefits of working with you.
- Sales don't happen overnight. It takes time for your customer to develop trust in you so keep in communication with them whether it is by email, newsletter, face-to-face, or by phone.

CHAPTER 5

The Customer-Centered Business Development Approach

Before we begin any strategizing for your P/S, we need to discuss how to build your business around your customer.

Whether you're in B2B (business-to-business) or B2C (business-to-consumer), besides your P/S, your customer is the most important part of your business. Without them, as you can imagine, there is no business. I've seen so many times that the small business entrepreneur forgets this. They focus solely on themselves, their P/S, and their bottom line and forget about the client/customer. A great customer experience should be your goal! That's what your competitors are doing!

Your unique customer experience. How do you see your customers reacting to your product? Excited? Inquisitive? This helps with your customer experience. Whether it's a point & click, it's someone coming into your store, or someone using your service by just speaking with you over phone, I would suggest thinking out the experience you would like the customer to have. This helps when you are planning and running your business.

WRITE IT DOWN: Sit and think about your customer. Who are they? What problem is your P/S going to solve for them? How is it going to make them FEEL?

Features vs. Benefits

Your messaging about your P/S has to "connect" with your customer. Using the features of your P/S to describe the benefits to your customer is a way to do that.

Features are the specifics of your P/S. Benefits are how your P/S helps the customer.

Let's say I've just come up with the most amazing idea ever. I've designed and manufactured a custom foot polisher (sorry, it's all I could come up with while writing this).

The features of my custom foot polisher are as follows:

- Automatic shut-off
- Comfortable hand held
- Delivered quickly

- Rechargeable
- Cordless
- Includes a nail customizer too!

So here's how to use the features to describe the benefits for your customer:

- Get smooth feet even in winter
- Perfect for that time between pedicures
- Makes your feet look smaller
- Turns off by itself so no fire hazard
- Saves money on batteries
- Makes your socks fit better
- Never get a run in your hose again!
- Look great in the summer without the salon trip!

The difference between features and benefits is that features are what the P/S is and benefits are how the P/S makes the life of your customer better. **These are the things you want to concentrate on in your marketing and sales strategy.** Again, exactly how does your customer get a fuzzy, warm feeling from your P/S? Does it bring them security? Does it save them money? Does it make them feel more secure? How does it help in a success for your customer? Your "HOW" is what will help define your messaging.

WRITE IT DOWN: In chapter 3 of the workbook, list out the features of your product or service first and then list out all the benefits of those features for your customers.

CHAPTER 6

Build Your Messaging

Before you have communication with your customers you have to determine what you are going to say. The goal of your messaging is to persuade your customer to buy your P/S. Your messaging directly supports your marketing objectives and strategy.

But luckily for you, you already know the features and benefits of your P/S. This is what all of your messaging is going to be crafted around. But first, let's talk a little about keywords.

Keywords are specific, descriptive words that are used to help your customer find your business online and satisfy search engine optimization (SEO) requirements. And why are we talking about this now? Because when you are crafting your message it's imperative that you realize that all of your content/messaging will be used to help increase the awareness and ranking of your business in search engines. So what are your keywords? Search for your P/S and your competitor's P/S on any of the major search engines (Google, Bing, or Yahoo). What are the words people use to search online when it comes to your P/S? Before you start to craft your messaging, make sure you know what keywords will work best to help potential customers find you in an Internet search. When you get to the website part of this book, I'll take you through how to use those keywords. Also, just an FYI, companies spend thousands of dollars trying to pinpoint exactly what keywords online users search in regards to their P/S. You can get free help with keywords online by searching "keyword search".

Once you have completed your keyword search (don't worry you can add or take away keywords later), the messaging you create from your keywords, benefits, and features will go on all promotional materials:

- Your and your employee's communication with customers and suppliers
- Marketing communications – website, brochures, email marketing
- Social media

Your messaging is already done, really. Take a look back at what you wrote in chapter 2 when you answered all those questions about your business. And then throw in what you wrote about your features and benefits.

Wait! You are a writer. Don't sell yourself short. I know, I know, the whole thought of writing something could be intimidating. But don't fret, you've got it in you, I know it.

Here are some guidelines:

- Use persuasive words like call, buy, win, sale, enjoy, get, etc.
- Always check your spelling and grammar.
- Keep your customer in mind while you are writing.
- Be conversational but avoid bad/negative words.
- Have any testimonials or customer experiences yet? Add them. (And when you get more, add them immediately).
- Build a story.
- Be precise. Most people don't have or want the time to read an entire liturgy on your P/S. They want the facts quickly, because that's how life is now: quick, quick, quick.
- Pretend that you have to pay $100 a word. This will help you make your copy as succinct as possible.
- Re-write. Yeah, re-writing can be horrible but will produce your best message. Best way to see it with fresh eyes is by putting it away for a few days and coming back to it. When you do come back to it, pretend you are the customer/employee/supplier when reading it.
- Never, ever be confrontational or condescending.

Remember, you want them to buy and feel good about it so they will tell their friends, family, and complete strangers how great you are.

- If you are truly stressed out by the thought of writing you can always hire someone to do it for you. You'll pay anywhere from $65-$125 an hour depending on who you select. You can post your job on Craigslist, Upwork, or Copyblogger. There are tons of sites that offer copywriting services. Make sure you get references and you settle on the deadline and the fee-per-hour or fee-per-project in writing.

- If you want to do it yourself, write what you would say to someone about your P/S (remember your one-minute elevator pitch?). You can always dictate your message into word via microphone and start from there. Have your friends and family read it, and give you feedback.

- Read it out loud. It will give you an idea of the flow of your writing. You can hear what's good and what's bad.

- For proofreading, again read it out loud and backwards. Here's the thing: if a customer finds a grammatical or spelling error in your messaging, you may be immediately discounted as a P/S they might purchase. It *doen't* (←typos are bad!) matter how amazing your offering is, you might lose a sale.

- Look at your competitor's websites, brochures, and any of their messaging. Of course, you'll want to differentiate yourself from your competition, but see what they did right and avoid what they did wrong.

WRITE IT DOWN:

There are many books to buy or borrow that can instruct you on exactly what words work best for the promotion of your P/S. I use *Words That Sell* by Richard Bayan and find it to be a good resource.

Also, if you don't have anyone who you trust to read through any of your business communications, I'll recommend S.C.O.R.E. again @ www.score.org. Or find a writing group. Almost every public library has one.

Fool around with your messaging. Say it as many ways as you can with as many keywords as you can cram in there. You know the benefits for your customer – you have the power to make them see, feel, and experience those benefits with your words. There are lots of ways to check your grammar and style on the web. Doing it yourself always saves time and money. Two websites that I'm familiar with are:

- Grammarly.com *
- Ginger.com*

*Please note that I have not used Grammarly.com (which I believe requires a fee) but I have used Ginger.com but only for grammar and spelling which was free.

CHAPTER 7

Building Your Brand with Marketing Communications

Marketing communications is the communication of your brand to your customers with media and messaging. Marketing communications are designed with your objectives and strategy in mind. The following is a list of some marketing communications:

- Websites
- Brochures
- Newsletters/ email communications
- Direct mail
- Coupons
- Presentations
- Business cards
- Social media

- Tradeshows
- Networking
- Mobile Strategy
- Digital banners
- Logos
- Your office/storefront
- Your signature on your business emails

TIP: All of your marketing communications should be similar in look and feel with consistent keyword infused messaging. Always include your logo, contact information, and website address on every piece of marketing that goes out the door. Remember, a similar look and feel helps your customer remember your brand.

Your Website

Just like your promotional plan, you should also have a website plan that will be a part of your larger business plan. In chapter 5 of the workbook you can craft your website plan.

Your Domain Name and Hosting Company

- Hosting companies often offer a way for you to register your domain name and sign up for hosting at the same time. Or you can register your domain name one place and then have it point to your hosting company. I find it's just easier to register the domain and get the hosting all in one place.

- Do you want your personal information private from anyone who wants to see who owns the domain? I have added security on all of my domain names. When you pay a little extra for privacy, you protect yourself from solicitations and hacking, which I consider a good investment.
- It is better for Search Engine Optimization (SEO) in the eyes of Google that you register your domain for three years or more.
- Hosting companies offer different options based on the size and needs of your website:
  - ➤ Shared hosting: good for the first-timer with an informational website without too many customers. Very cost efficient. Disk space and bandwidth is limited.
  - ➤ Managed Wordpress hosting: more expensive than shared, this is specifically formulated for Wordpress websites.
  - ➤ Dedicated: good for ecommerce, security, and a large customer base. More expensive than Shared.
  - ➤ Cloud/VPS hosting: better security and speed. A larger business with an extensive customer base and an ecommerce website would likely use this.

Here are a few of the more popular hosting companies (there

are a ton of them out there - these are the one's that I've had experience with):

- Bluehost
- Godaddy
- Amazon Web services
- Network Solutions

So based on your website plan, choose the hosting company that combines the best price, uptime, and features that will best suit your objectives and strategy.

Other questions that need to be answered in a website plan:

- What is your domain name?
    - When you register your domain name, make sure you get a .com address. That's what resonates with people. Also, make it as short and sweet as possible.
- What kind of content are you going to have on your site?
    - ➢ Words
    - ➢ Videos
    - ➢ Images
- Where will you get that content?

Website Content

- Videos. If you want your website to open with a video, there are many stock video options available for

purchase. Some websites that offer stock video and photography are:
- ➢ https://www.istockphoto.com/
- ➢ https://www.gettyimages.com

- If you are using Wordpress, you can buy a theme that will probably include free video and image content. Again, stock photography sites offer images, icons, logos, and videos. Always look at the license about using the work personally or commercially.
- Is your site informational or are you selling through your website?
  - ➢ If you are selling through your website, how are you going to set that up? Through my hosting company, I can set my e-commerce site up with Wordpress and they make it look pretty easy. So, again, examine your hosting company carefully to make sure that you are getting exactly what you need in terms of website functionality for your business.
- What are the different sections of the site?
  - ➢ Common top menu sections are About, Services, Shop, Blog, Contact us
- List out all the pages of your site. I find it's a good idea to use a flow chart to visually see all of your pages under your sections. It really helps when you are designing or explaining to a designer what you want.
- Look at your competition – what are they doing?

- What is the action you want your customer to take?
  - Sign up
  - Buy/order
  - Call
  - Visit
- How are you going to gather the names and email addresses of your site visitors to create an email list?
  - In the email marketing section of this book, I will introduce you to the two email newsletter programs that offer a way for you to gather email addresses for your customer list.
- Are you going to design it yourself, use the online designer that comes with your hosting company, or hire an outside company?
  - In Wordpress?
  - HTML?
  - Another programming language?
- What is the launch date?

There are other options for all-in-one website hosting, domain name registration, and website design that can offer you the whole package.

- Wix
- Squarespace
- Website Builder
- Godaddy, Bluehost

Often when you sign up for hosting you get the option of using the website builder included with your service. This can be very beneficial in saving you time and money, so before you sign up for a hosting service, ask all about what's included in your hosting fee. Usually, these website builders provide an easy, educational way to learn about website design. The hosting company WANTS to help you because that means you'll spend money with them so don't be afraid to ask for their assistance.

And if I may say, these days it is really easy to design your website yourself. Having been a professional web designer in the past, I believe that you shouldn't be intimidated by the thought of designing your own website. It's much easier than you think and designing it yourself will give you more control and save money.

Some common web design practices:

- A call to action goes in the upper right corner of your top menu. Like **"Buy Now"** or **"Donate here"** or **"Call us"** or **"Sign up"**. And it works best in red with black or white font.

- **Best font for your website?** Stay away from lofty, complex fonts that seem to float. A quick font lesson: a Serif font (like Times, Garamond, or Georgia) is best for printed communications and a Sans-Serif font (like Arial, Verdana, or Helvetica) is best for online communications. You want to use the simplest font for people to read. **Remember, you have seven seconds to keep your audience's attention before they**

move on to your competitor. So an easy-to-read sans-serif font is a good choice for the main font of your website.

- **Maximize your front page.** What information does your customer want to know? I'm always amazed that on restaurant websites that the first thing I don't see is the hours, menu, location, and great reviews right on the front page. Because scratch-n-sniff for the Internet hasn't been invented yet, those three things are the most important that I want to see when I'm looking for food. Then if I have the time to hang around, you can tell me more about your chef, catering options, or whatever else you feel is most important to persuade me to dine here.

- **Remember your messaging.** Many times your content will determine your design. Is your site image or video heavy? If I can give a little advice, based on the seven second rule, present your P/S benefit/feature messaging in bullet points. People don't have a lot of time to read paragraphs of information.

- **Don't forget about a mobile strategy!** I know I'm just touching on this, but make sure your website works seamlessly on your phone. If you are using Wordpress for your site, it allows you to see how exactly your website will look and function on your phone or tablet. When you are discussing your site with your designer, please make sure you understand how your website will function on tablets and phones.

Your Website and Search Engine Optimization (SEO)

Everyone wants to be on the first page of search results when someone looks for their business. And you can pay a lot of money to get there. Don't have a lot of that yet? Well, I've got some good hacks to help you get as high as you can for maximum exposure.

> **Remember that your website is your little piece of real estate on the big Internet. Maximize your presence as much as possible.**

Keywords

This in one of the most important aspects of SEO and website design. As I touched on earlier, keywords are words and phrases that an online user may use to search for your business in Google/Yahoo/Bing. When these specific words are used in a search and you have placed them in the content of your site, you are more apt to show up close to the top of search results, making it easier for a potential sale to find you. (You can also pay to reach the top of search results – check out Google Adwords if that is something you'd like explore). If you have designed your site in HTML, you will add your elevator pitch (description) and your keywords to a section of your code called "Meta name". Search online for "how to add keywords to your HTML or Wordpress site" and you will find many tutorials on how to do it.

You need to make sure that you put your keywords in the following places:

- ➢ Page titles
- ➢ Headlines
- ➢ Content

Other ways to increase your page ranking on search engines:

1. Always have a footer with a menu on your website
2. Always include a site map section of your website
3. Google does not recognize images or videos as keywords, so if your website is image/video heavy, you'll need to make sure you include keywords in other places on your site.
4. Update your website as much as you can because Google hates stale websites!
5. When your website is complete, check the 'time-to-load' by typing your domain name into a website speed site. Search for 'Check time to load' and pick a free site. (I use Pingdom and it always works for me).
6. Test. Test. Test. When you think you are done, have some friends or family test your site on their phones, tablets, and laptops. Always test your site on various browsers.

Your Brochure

There are many different ways of crafting your brochure – easily at home or you can have a graphic design company or professional printer do it for you.

- Single sheet, Tri-fold (most popular), Bi-fold (This is one

8.5x11 sheet folded and can be printed by you)
- 4 page 11 x 17 (you'll need a printer for this)

It's fine for your brochure to be in black and white so if that's what you can do starting out then do it!

I recently attended the NY Auto Show and a large majority of automakers do not offer anything on paper anymore. If you want to save paper and trees (and money), just use your website as your brochure or create your brochure digitally and offer it over social media, email, and on your website.

Printing your brochure yourself you will need:

- A good home printer
- A publishing program that you probably already have!
  - Microsoft Publisher or Word – you will probably already have these programs on your computer and they are easy to use. You can search for brochure templates from thousands of samples and customize one for your business and save it as a PDF or print it yourself.
  - Adobe Illustrator or InDesign – just an FYI – if you don't know the Adobe programs, learning them can be quite time consuming. Should you want to pursue learning how to use them, buy or borrow a book and download the thirty-day free trial and have at it! You can buy any Adobe product a month-at-a-time so as far as an monetary

investment it's minimal.

> There are also free online design resources such as Pixabay (free images), Gimp (design), and Canva (images and design).

You can also design your brochure using an online printer. I have used Vistaprint numerous times and have found them to be a reliable and successful option for a printer. There are many different options for online printers so check the reviews and make a selection.

The tri-fold brochure is one of the most popular sizes of brochure that you can create. They are small and easy to print and don't take up a lot of room on a tradeshow table or countertop. On the outside will be your front cover, back cover and inside flap. On the front cover you want your most important information (why should your customer read your brochure?), on the contact page should be all of your contact information and your call-to-action, and on the inside flap you want your benefit bullet points. Definitely use images and charts – it makes it easier for people to read. Make sure that you have the same look and feel as your other marketing communication pieces. See the templates on the following two pages for dimensions and panel details.

Tri-fold Brochure Outside

Product/Service Benefits Bulletpoints Panel 3.688" Width	Contact Information Back Cover 3.688" Width	Logo Tag line Front Cover 3.688" Width

Tri-fold Brochure Inside

The inside of the brochure lays flat when opened up so don't worry about designing across the whole page.
You get more design options for designing across the page. I have designed many brochures this way.

Panel #1	Panel #2	Panel #3
3.688" Width	3.688" Width	3.625" Width

Outsourcing your Brochure

- A professional graphic designer can run you between $65 - $125+ an hour. A typical brochure project can run anywhere between 5-20+ hours depending on your requirements. When dealing with a graphic designer, make sure you get all the specifications from that graphic designer before you begin (this will save the graphic designer time and you money), provide your content without typos, your pictures are high resolution (300 pixels-per-inch or PPI), and anything else they request. The more content you provide for the graphic designer, the quicker they will be able to create the design for you and the cheaper it will be. Always make sure that you get the final files from the graphic designer as well as a PDF to use on your website and to send to potential clients. Please make sure you have all deadline dates in writing and you negotiate the price for the project before you enter into any contractual relationship with a graphic designer. Also, if you are dealing with a local printer, your graphic designer should be able to work with them.

- A local, professional printer. Many printers also provide graphic design services. The printers that I have dealt with charge $125 an hour for those services. It's an easy option because they will design and print your brochure and you get to use a local business! (That's always good).

If you are outsourcing your brochure, make sure you know the requirements for the file like image resolution, Pantone color, and size requirements. Also, you are responsible for any typos in your brochure that need to be corrected. <u>The printer is not responsible for typos or grammatical errors.</u>

How to avoid the evil typo in your final print? Whether you are doing it yourself, hiring a graphic designer, or using the design services of a local or online printer, YOU ARE RESPONSIBLE FOR YOUR OWN CONTENT. Make sure that your content is typo and grammar mistake free! Read the content out loud and backwards and then bribe your assistant (or significant other/kid/friend) to do the same thing. Your graphic designer or printer may miss something. At the end of the project and before the final print you will be provided with a proof of the final design that you can check and recheck for typos. You will then have to approve it for final print. Even with online printers you have to approve the proof for any typos or grammatical errors.

Email Newsletters

Small business owners often produce both hard copy and email newsletters for their customers.

A hard copy printed or PDF newsletter is easy to produce in any of the publishing programs listed in the previous section and can be printed and snail-mailed or emailed directly to your customer list as a PDF. Many small business owners find success doing a digital newsletter and it is a cost effective strategy for those just starting out.

An email newsletter is also an easy way to engage with potential customers. Once you have finalized your branding design (font, messaging, images, colors), just apply the same design and messaging that you used on your brochure and website. Consistency is key!

Even if you don't have a huge email list to begin with, you can still pass your newsletter – whether as PDF or as an email – out to potential customers. Post it to your social media accounts and send it to everyone you know on your email list – customers, friends, family, or previous colleagues and even suppliers.

How do you get people to subscribe to your email list? By offering something for free. Some examples include a coupon, free eBook, recipe, menu plan, or a P/S introduction video. Offer some kind of helpful information to your customers and they will sign up in a second.

Idea time! What "*Free*" thing can you offer your customer in exchange for their email/name/address/phone that totally benefits their life, makes them feel good about you, and turns them into a customer, friend, or partner?

Don't forget to load up your newsletter with your keywords because again, anything loaded with keywords helps your Internet/digital marketing strategy to get a higher ranking in Google. And don't forget to read it aloud or backwards to flush out any typos.

How to design and distribute your email newsletter? First, if you have no money whatsoever, you can design it in MS Word, save out as a PDF, and then email, social media, and text your newsletter to your customer list.

Email Newsletter Design

Most email newsletters are cut into four sections.

- Top
- Mid-top
- Center
- Bottom

The top is where your logo or business name goes. It's also where – if you are sending an unsolicited email to a list – you insert the term "Advertisement" or "Solicitation" above your logo.

The mid-top is where you might put a graphic or text describing what your newsletter is about.

The center is where your written content resides.

The bottom is your call-to-action, contact information, and social media links.

Email newsletter design is an art and a science. You can use as many images as you like and most people keep their newsletters very simple. To me, it's really a way for your P/S to stay in the front of your customer's mind.

Just search "best email newsletters" and you will get a slew of examples.

As for professional newsletter programs, Mailchimp offers a free option for you to use. Mailchimp is free for any business that has less than 2000 subscribers and offers numerous benefits in the free category. After you exceed your 2000 subscribers, your price is $10/month.

There's also Constant Contact but it's a bit pricier. They offer a 60 day free trial (without a credit card) and after that it's $20/month for 0-500 subscribers and after you reach 500+ subscribers it's $45 a month.

I have used both programs to market products and services and both have their pros and cons. Research the reviews and try designing your newsletter in both and see which one you like best. Always apply your branding to your newsletter so it has the same look and feel as all of your other communications.

Newsletter Ideas

- Grand opening
- New P/S offerings
- Client testimonials

- A how-to instructional post
- How your P/S helps people
- A customer success story
- Upcoming events where your customers can meet you
- Promotions/coupons
- An online survey of your P/S with a giveaway of a $25 Amazon gift card
- New talent acquisitions

Your newsletter doesn't always have to be about business! When I designed a newsletter for that tax company, I would always add a section that was interesting but not tax related. One month I wrote about vacation ideas for stressed-out accountants. I had many customers – most of whom I had never met personally – come to me at tradeshows to mention how much they liked my newsletter. Remember, reading your newsletter should bring something to the reader's party, or else you'll end up in the spam bin or the unthinkable: unsubscribed!

Always include a way to buy your service or product in your newsletter or any customer email. Ask for the sale!!!

Landing pages/strategy: A landing page is a specific page on your website dedicated to a link attached to your email newsletter (or digital banner). Use a landing page in conjunction with a link in your newsletter with a promotion. Mailchimp has such a service or you can design one yourself in Wordpress or whatever program used to design your site. Remember, as with your website, your landing page should have a similar look and feel and always put the call-to-action you want most – a donation, purchase, call – in red or some other contrasting color up in the right-hand corner.

With Constant Contact and Mailchimp, you can track exactly who is opening, not opening, or unsubscribing from your newsletter.

Don't forget to post your newsletter to your website and social media sites! And, here's a tip, turn each newsletter into a blog post for your website.

Let's talk about marketing lists for a moment: first of all, honestly, buying an unsolicited email list is a risky proposition. The odds of ending up in your customer's inbox, as opposed to their SPAM box, are pretty low. But look up the pros and cons and see if it's for you. I have tried it for one business and I had an 11% open rate. Was that worth the price of the list? No, it wasn't. If you are interested in purchasing a list for an email campaign please take a look at the estimated open rate. You'll want to look for an 80-85% accuracy rate. That is the rate of emails in the list that are correct and will hopefully reach the inbox of your potential customer.

If you are sending an unsolicited email to a list, you need to label that email correctly to include the words "Advertisement" or "Solicitation", have your physical address, and provide an opt-out for your subscribers.

> **For more information on unsolicited business email rules, search for the CAN SPAM Act of 2003.**

Direct Mail

Direct mail is not dead. Check your mailbox and you will see (especially from restaurants and realtors) a lot of examples of direct mail. Addresses are easy to obtain and if you buy a list from a list source, most business or consumer addresses will be included. And, unlike an email list, you have a much higher delivery rate with physical addresses.

You can design a piece of direct mail yourself (but always have it professionally printed), use a graphic designer/Internet printer, a local printer/list management company or a company that designs and mails coupons for you like Clipper or Valpak. And many companies will design, mail with postage, and track your direct mail piece for you. Remember to use your branding to make sure everything is the same! If you are using a postcard as your direct mail piece, make sure it's a big size (generally 8.5x5) or else it will literally get lost in the mail.

Some ideas for your direct mail piece:

- Call-to action (buy, call, visit)
- Pictures of your product/establishment/customer
- Introduction and benefits of your P/S for your customer
- A name/phone/email/address/web address

- Instructions to go to a landing page
- Coupon or Promotion (most used by restaurants, contractors)
- Location of upcoming event with the opportunity to meet

Other marketing communications that need consistent branding:

- Coupons
- Presentations
- Digital banners
- Tradeshow handouts/booth design
- Mobile strategy
- Social media

In chapter 5 of the workbook, you can sketch out your ideas for your website, brochure, and email newsletter.

CHAPTER 8

Tradeshow Strategies

Tradeshows (with the right audience) are a good place to find pre-qualified customers. A tradeshow provides you with an opportunity to get up close and personal with new customers and to make initial connections that could possibly turn strangers into customers. Some tradeshows even offer you – for an extra fee – to get time with the most prequalified customers that you can find.

Finding Your Dream Tradeshow

Does your P/S benefit a customer who is a member of an industry specific organization? If you provide a service to a professional industry, there will be many sponsorship/tradeshow opportunities with the possibility of getting you in front of your optimal lead. Look at your customer segment – is your segment heavy with accountants/ lawyers/doctors/any professional industry – there are tons of sponsorship opportunities where you can network. Believe me, people love being part of an organization.

Recently I did a project for a company that provides additional tax services for Certified Public Accountants. Except for the months between January and April, CPAs like to hang out at continuing education professional tax seminars. These seminars are provided by a state CPA organization and they provided numerous sponsorship opportunities for the company (ranging in price from $300 to $1000 per seminar) as well as seminar and tradeshow opportunities to interact with CPAs. There was also a golf outing where our logo was prominently displayed and that cost about $1000.

Before you pay for most tradeshows, you should be able to select your booth number and see it on the tradeshow floor map. Hint: try and get on the main isle of the floor. A good place is at the main entrance or anywhere around where people are eating. An end cap is very good because you get coverage from more than one side. Look at the map and see where the main thoroughfare is or where attendees will congregate in groups – you'll get a good amount of traffic there. If the company can not provide a map, please get some idea of where you are going to be and if possible, see who your neighbors are.

Do your research. I have to say that many tradeshows are duds and sometimes, it's hard to figure that out ahead of time. Best way to protect yourself is to really study the previous attendee list if you can get one. Also, ask your friends/mentors/colleagues, and see where your competition is exhibiting and do online research. Look at reviews and what others are saying. Also, if you want to do a tradeshow and get an optimum booth in a great area, you have to start early - like sometimes a year to six months before the tradeshow. So call as early as you can!

Relationship idea! If you get a current attendee list for your selected tradeshow, select 5-10 people that you want to meet. Drop them an email, postcard, or call introducing yourself and your P/S. When you see them during the show see if you can set up a meeting time or buy them coffee.

And just an FYI, tradeshows can be time consuming and expensive and sometimes you don't get any sales traction from them whatsoever. Research! Research! Research! You want to make sure that your time and monetary investment are going to pay off!

For example: the company that I worked for usually charged between $3000 and up for their service. The tradeshow cost was $2000 and if I got one job (which I did) then the tradeshow paid for itself and I get a lot of free networking opportunities. And I got into the front of the minds of people who were future customers.

If you are looking for something a little smaller and you have a consumer product, there are plenty of smaller local tradeshows where you can exhibit. Look at local chambers of commerce for opportunities, your local Rotary, or your local school. Your town may have business associations that you can join. Here where I live in Monmouth County, New Jersey, we have a "Made in Monmouth" festival put on by the local county. There are 4h fairs that run statewide in the summer. **Get an idea of where your customers will want to pay to go and then be there.**

What do you do once you've found your tradeshow? Many tradeshow deposits are not refundable and can be a sizable percentage of the overall tradeshow price, so make sure that you have a backup attendee should something keep you from being there.

Review your table size. At the smaller tradeshows you will generally be paying for a 10 x 10 booth that includes a table, two chairs, and standard carpeting.

What will cost extra:

- Electrical outlets
- Digital lead reader (sometimes this is included in price)
- Extra nice carpeting
- Garbage cans
- Cleaners to clean the booth and empty garbage each day of the show
- Additional furniture

- Wireless Internet
- Booth Assembly – for bigger booths

Tradeshow set up:

- Make sure you understand the set up and break down of your booth. Many smaller tradeshows let you register and show up, get directions to your booth, and set your stuff up easy peasy. But if you have a larger booth that requires construction, you may have to use unions to help you with your set up. So, here's what I learned about working with unions: do not touch anything until you check in with the union representative at the front. Have a clear set of directions when you arrive for the carpeting, electrical, Internet, and booth assembly. And, be nice to the union workers because they are the ones who are going to get you all set up. You will deal with the electrician, carpet installer, and general construction manager. They are a helpful group and I really relied on them for getting my large booth set up. In the end I was glad they were there and really appreciated their help. (I also brought them coffee).
- Setting your booth up yourself. Bring a cart or something that you can carry everything in one trip from your car or your hotel room. And please bring shoes that still look nice but you don't mind walking or standing in for a long time. A long trip in uncomfortable business shoes is no

fun. (If you have too much you can always ship your stuff before the tradeshow – just give yourself enough time for your booth to get there!) Upon check in at the registration desk, make your way to your booth (which you already know because it's on your floor map). Pick up your digital lead reader if you got one.

TIP: Always take a picture of your booth before the attendees arrive. That way if you need to recreate what worked or change something that didn't, you'll have something to work from. And you can post it on Twitter, Instagram, and Facebook and invite people to come.

Before the tradeshow begins:

- Dress for success. No jeans. Preferably a suit for men or a suit/dress for women or a uniform of logo'd Polo shirt/khakis if you are at a B2B tradeshow. At a B2C tradeshow, make sure that you are dressed appropriately. The no jeans rule applies here too. Don't worry about what your neighbors are wearing. Just dress nice – it makes a difference.
- Make friends with your neighbors. Work together. They may have customers that will use your P/S and you maybe able to push customers to them as well. And you'll have someone to talk to during any downtime or when there are evening events.
- Walk the floor with your business cards during downtimes. See where your competitors are and what

type of swag they are offering. Talk to them – there's business for everyone! Befriend them – but not too much, you know? Don't give away any secrets. Who else is there? Anyone that you would be interested in converting to a partner? If you do leave your booth, make sure that you secure any raffle prize or electronics that you have at your booth. Unfortunately, I've been at tradeshows where people have been ripped off.

Make sure at your booth you have:

- A giveaway where you collect business cards in exchange for a raffle: I used to give away the Kindle Fire. I would spend about $50 but the customer who won always remembered me!
- A sign explaining your giveaway.
- A fishbowl to collect business cards.
- I always have a pad/pen available for those people who don't have business cards. They still get an entry and you still get their information.
- Mints: first, people stop and get mints, and second, your breath is always minty fresh! Only big lifesavers not candy! Mints have a totally different persona!
- Some kind of logo'd takeaway: squish balls, pen/pad, something related to your P/S: Idea day think about!
- Your brochures and your postcards that you sent out. If you put a coupon on the postcard make sure you offer

that to people at the tradeshow.
- You will probably have some sort of digital lead collector – use it!

During the tradeshow:

- Smile and be excited! People don't stop to talk to people who aren't making eye contact or smiling. And not everyone is going to stop at your booth because not everyone needs what you are selling. Focus on the people that do stop and talk to you.
- Recognize the conversationalists. There will be some sales guys masquerading as possible customers that stop and talk to you. They will keep talking even after you've moved on to real customers. Recognize these people, ask for their card and tell them you'll consider it (or say you don't need it) and move them along.
- Have any existing customers attending the tradeshow? Look them up and plan a meeting time. Take them to lunch or bring them some of your swag and your coupon.
- If you get a good lead by meeting someone, take their business card, and email or text (or their preferred communication) within 10 minutes with a future meeting, a call, a promotion, or whatever it is you're giving away.
- Hand out your business cards.
- Strike up conversations.
- Stand in front or the side of your booth. You're more

accessible that way.

- Hand out your brochures and your swag.
- If you are selling product online to either B2B or B2C, have your website available on a tablet or laptop for easy ordering.
- Listen! Your customer will tell you what they want!
- Take notes. During any downtimes, take notes on future meetings, add leads to CRM, or perfect your message based on any customer feedback you've gotten.
- There may be extra networking events in the evening. Take advantage of these. You may be able to get in front of some great potential leads. Do yourself a favor though: don't drink. I've seen some people blow customer trust by imbibing way too much. And it really ruins your next day, because no one wants to be hung-over. Also, get in and get out – talk to as many people as possible, watch what you eat (no spinach, garlic, and bring some of your mints) and excuse yourself after you eat to check your teeth.
- Choose your giveaway winner and contact them about winning.
- If your tradeshow is wrapping up soon, go to registration and confirm your shipping information.

Tradeshow breakdown:

- You wouldn't believe how easy break down is! It will go

fast. Try and pack your most important lead information where you can access it while you are flying home. That way you can review and make plans.
- Make sure you leave your neighbors with your business cards and plan or confirm any partner meeting that you may have.
- Go return your digital lead reader and confirm how you will get those leads – email/text?
- See if you can get a final attendee list emailed to you – if not confirm a date with the tradeshow company when that will come.

After the tradeshow:

- You have seven days to contact your leads or else your competition will!
- Confirm any new client meetings that you set up during the show.
- Send a "Sorry we missed you email" to any potential leads that you missed and offer them 25% off or another promotion.
- Follow up with any outstanding potential leads
- Follow up with an email newsletter to everyone who entered your giveaway
- Take any customer feedback and strengthen your message

Put your stuff away and get back to work!

CHAPTER 9

Social Media

Social media can be a cost effective way for your small business to engage and resonate with customers and a great way to build your brand.

The secret to social media success?

- Interesting content
- Frequency
- Engagement with your customers
- Consistency

The more you use social media for your business, the more it will grow and give you a return on your time. With social media you definitely get out what you put into it. Social media can help you establish yourself as an authority about your P/S and increase the level of trust that customers need in order to purchase from you.

Users of social media by age:

- LinkedIn: 30-49 (average) | 500 million users
- Twitter: 18-29 | 328 million users
- Facebook: 40-65 | 2 billion users
- Snapchat: child-19 | 187 million users
- Instagram: 18-34 | 800 million users

Based on your market, that might give you an idea of where to focus your social media promotion efforts. There are many other social media outlets available; I'm just focusing on the ones that I have used.

Check your competitors! Are they on social media? Why not? Sometimes social media doesn't make sense. But, even if your competitors aren't on there, maybe you should be. There may be a hidden market that you can attack with your ingenuity that your competitor might miss.

Think about why your customers come to social media sites. Many times it's really just to see if they can get you to engage with them. I say do it. People feel special when they reach out to you and you reach back. Really, they love it. Other times it's to complain, check on events, or just to see what's happening.

Twitter: Tweet Your Way to Business Success

To start using Twitter: go on, sign up, and get yourself an account – it's easy! When setting up your account profile use your keywords in the description, which will help your Twitter feed be found in Google search results – and pick a good Twitter handle because once you decide on that, you can't change it. You can also use hashtags in your profile so your account can be found easier in Twitter, (hashtags can be used on almost every single social media account). Hashtags are metatags that allow you to easily find messages with the same content or theme. It allows groups of people to tweet about and find content on the same topic. On my profile I use the hashtags #amwriting and #businessdevelopment. When people search for either of those hashtags, my profile comes up in the search.

Just an FYI and I know we are focusing on small business here but if you look at larger companies like Apple – it's never tweeted anything and yet has almost 2 million followers. Amazon tweets daily, with an emphasis on how their products or services can help people. They have almost 3 million users and only follow 35.

What to post on Twitter? Your latest blog posts, newsletters, engage with followers (answer a question about your P/S), post something funny (be careful here – people are quick to be offended by stuff), a piece of timely news that affects your P/S (like when sports betting was approved in NJ, our local racetrack tweeted how great they thought it was and how it would affect the hours of the race track, etc.).

Pinned tweets: a pinned tweet is a tweet that sits at the top of your Twitter feed and is the first tweet someone sees when they look at your profile. A good example of a pinned tweet would be whatever the most important post that you have right now – a promotion or a new product or something that people will find interesting about your business. If you want to "Pin" a tweet just go to that tweet, when you hover over the tweet you'll see an arrow in the upper right hand corner and select "Pin Tweet to profile page" and that will do it. Change your Pinned tweets with each new blog post or, really, any new event or P/S offering – you don't want your Twitter feed getting stale!

How do you get Twitter followers?

- You can buy followers – which I would not do. You want to grow your followers organically. Many times when you buy followers they are fake.
- You follow other people. I had the opportunity to meet an up and coming author once and she boasted that she had all of these Twitter followers but never followed anyone back. I feel that that's kind of limiting. When you follow someone – a customer or a supplier – they feel a little jolt of "oh, cool, they followed me." It's like camaraderie and another way to engage with your customer. And you don't have to follow everyone. Be picky about who you follow! Sometimes people post things that may be of questionable nature to you that you might not want associated with your business. And people are going to look at who you follow. So when someone

follows you – please go on their Twitter account and check out their tweets. If someone is tweeting something that you find questionable, then don't follow them. Also, you can easily block people if you need to.

What you want on Twitter is for as many followers to retweet your tweet to their followers so you get more followers. Confusing? It won't be once you start using it. You can also post pictures/details of your P/S and tag followers. To tag a follower, just add their handle to your tweet like @L_Ann_Dyer.

Twitter is an intimate way for you to interact directly with your customers. You can direct message (DM) people or tweet right to them.

Whenever you get a follower, always, always, always thank them. Send out a tweet (with their handles included like @L_Ann_Dyer) to multiple followers telling them how much you appreciate their follow. This is a good engagement tactic and will likely get you retweeted to their followers.

Be careful what you retweet! Sometimes a retweet will signal to people that you "endorse" that person or P/S that you retweeted. But always retweet shout-outs, positive reviews, or any other positive information people post about you. Thank the user for doing that - it will go a long way.

Advertising on Twitter: Many bigger companies advertise on Twitter with promoted tweets or promoted follows. You can have Twitter promote your tweets or you can perform an entire ad campaign on Twitter. A Twitter promotion campaign will run you $99/month and ad campaigns are "Pay per click" using a monthly budget that you set.

Please weigh the ROI on a Twitter campaign. For local and smaller businesses, I'm not completely sold on advertising on Twitter.

Facebook: Connect with over 2 billion Users

Well, you probably won't connect with the entire 2 billion but you can expose your business to a fraction of it. Facebook, like Twitter, requires frequency, dedication, a sense of humor, and patience. Facebook can be your permanent space on the web or can be a part of your overall marketing strategy. You want to post on Facebook how great your P/S is, stories of how you are helping your customer, check it daily for messages from your customer, and add lots of original content to it – videos, photos, messages, anecdotes, instructions for using your P/S, something that complements your P/S, use Facebook Live, and add your story using Facebook Story.

Facebook is essentially free for you to use starting out for your business and it can be a great tool for connecting to your customers on a daily basis. (But we must remember that we can't get caught up in all the cute French bulldog videos or animations of babies playing orchestral instruments - GUILTY!)

Let's set up your Facebook page for your business:

1. You have to have a personal Facebook account to have a Facebook "Page" for your business. That way you are the "administrator" of the page and the page is attached to your account.
2. On the left of your personal page there will be a section called "Pages". Click on that and you will be taken to main pages list.
3. Up in the right corner you will see a green button that says "Create Page". Select that and choose "Business or Brand" and click on the gray "Get Started" button.
4. Add your business name and then select a category. When selecting a category, you have to start typing and categories will show up.
5. That will take you to a page where you can add a profile picture – which should be a picture of your logo or some other corresponding image that is associated with your brand. Then you have the opportunity to add a cover photo – this is the large photo across the top.
6. Once you have added your photos, you will be at your page where you will have the opportunity to invite your friends. DO IT! Invite everyone you know. Promote yourself!
7. Add your business description (use your keywords here), add a button, send people to your website, and you can even create a group for your page! If you are totally new

to Facebook, please read the page tips - they are a quick and easy read! On your Facebook page you can add a button for bookings/appointments, one to contact you, one for learning more about your business, shopping with you, or to download an app or game.

Facebook Groups: I'm a member of a number of groups on Facebook – some promoting something and others just for people looking for like-minded friends or support. You can create your group in the "Page Tips" area and add a personal message and invite people you know. Groups are a great way to promote your business while engaging people to write about their feelings about your P/S. It's also a great place to answer customer questions. If you can, set up a group for your business, it can lead to an increase in sales!

You now have your Facebook page set up for your customers! Now, what to post?

- Post a welcome message
- If you decide to do Facebook Live, tweet out to your followers that they can see you there!
- Photos of your P/S in action
- Just as an FYI: Facebook recently changed its algorithm so that posts with more comments are more likely to show up in your follower's newsfeed than posts without comments. Page posts that get people talking will get more exposure and what gets the most exposure are

videos, positive customer discussions around your business, or increased engagement from events. Facebook Live is a great way to get the discussion moving around a particular topic and garners lots of comments, likes and views.

- **Facebook Stories:** Just like SnapChat and Intagram, Facebook Stories allows you to share original content. Your "Story" can be created on your phone and uploaded to your page for 24 hours and then (so they say) will disappear forever. A great idea for the small business would be to create a video of yourself at an event or in your store and tell a product story.

Idea Day: Come up with 10 posts for your social media accounts and a social media calendar of post dates.

Instagram: pictures that promote

Got a camera? Then you can succeed at Instagram. It's easy to set up your account (I won't through it here – I mean it's really easy) and then just start snapping.

- Have a brick and mortar store? Snap pictures of your favorite customers and post to FB/TW/ and Instagram for them to be an instant hit. But ask first!
- Follow other people – friends, customers, suppliers, even your competitors
- Pictures of your town
- Photos of a charity you are supporting

- Pictures of you and your customers at events (Again, whenever posting a picture of someone, please get their permission)
- Pictures of your suppliers
- Anything that will entertain and capture your existing and potential customer's attention is good

As with Facebook, you can create stories with your Instagram account. When you login into the Instagram App, you will see "Stories" on the top of the screen. Click on that and create your story!

Never, ever, ever (can I say that again?) post anything negative on social media. It will hurt you and your business. And forget politics, too. Save those for your personal accounts. And even then, I would be careful. First of all, when I'm somewhere on Facebook where it's supposed to be about let's say, old houses, and someone (usually not the admin) posts something about politics, I am immediately turned off. Remember, this is business and that's what you should stick too.

Remember for social media – frequent, original, and engaging content is what people want. Even if your product is plumbing pipes or your service is toenail cleaning (nothing wrong with either of those but they're no electric car or celebrity dog walking service, you know?), original, engaging content will increase the awareness of your brand on social media.

CHAPTER 10

Your CRM – The Personal Assistant That You Really Need

Customer Relationship Management (CRM) is a software tool that keeps track of all of the customer communications, service calls, project dates, invoices - really, anything that has to do with the customer service and communication of your business. It keeps track of your marketing program, sales achievements, and the changing sales process. You keep informed about calls that need to be made, upcoming meetings, where customers are in the lead/customer/project process, and allows you to access your customers details all in one place. I meet so many small business owners that don't have a CRM. They automatically think it's too hard to set up or too expensive! Nothing could be farther from the truth. CRMs are an important tool that increases your chance of business success!

Why do you need one? A CRM frees up your mind to concentrate on the core of your business, which is your P/S. It is helpful having your customer information all in one place to easily reach for when you need it. Don't let this information get away by not having a CRM!

Want to go really cheap? Just use an Excel file to keep track of all of your customer information. Set up the following columns in Excel (for possible import later) and use the file daily (or as much as you can):

- Contact name
- Company name
- Address
- Address #2
- City
- State
- Zip
- Phone
- Cell phone
- Email
- Website
- Facebook
- Twitter
- Instagram

- Other social media sites
- Social media interactions/comments
- Notes
- Initial communication
- Date of last communication
- Previous emails
- Previous phone discussions
- Upcoming call dates
- Numbers of products ordered
- Product purchase date
- Order price
- Price per piece
- Service date
- Service completion date
- Service issues
- Customer service issues?
- Issue solved how?

Which CRM to choose?

If you want to go with a paid solution, I have used ZOHO for small business but there are many others out there that are just as good. Zoho is an excellent choice if you are just starting out because it is very simple to set up and use and can cost as little as $12 a month per-user. Research and read reviews on the CRM that's best for you.

Setting up a solution like Zoho or one of the other smaller

options is very easy.

First, if you have data to import, you can import it in the set up section of your CRM.

Do you have existing data already in an Excel customer file? You can easily import that and automatically have the CRM populated with your data. The columns in your Excel file will correspond with the 'Fields' in your CRM. So if you have columns like the ones I describe in the previous section, that's the data that will be populated.

Just an FYI for when you import your data: Match the 'Account' field in the CRM with the 'Company' field in your Excel file. For some reason CRMs prefer "Account" over "Company".

How much information do you need about a customer? Maybe it's just their email address. I know a few companies that use their email newsletter software as their CRM. But it's limiting and you can only keep track of newsletter information and not the overall communication with customers.

Recently I had the opportunity to set up a CRM for a small software business that produced reports for customers. It had two different segments:

- B2B – (business-to-business) corporate customers who would be purchasing multiple reports over an extended period of time.

- B2C – (business-to-consumer) one-off private consumers who would sign up to buy one report and then leave and never return.

Now this business owner was not doing anything with the B2C customer data as he had yet to see the benefit of manipulating that data. I suggested a segment specific email newsletter along with a specific social media channel detailing report improvements that were coming in the following months to the consumer segment.

How do you get the contacts/leads/accounts to fill your CRM?

- Email marketing software
- You can buy a list of potential customers to contact from a direct marketing list
- Many CRMs have a sign up form feature that allows you to collect data directly from your website.
- Tradeshows
- Networking groups
- Referrals
- Facebook/Twitter/Instagram
- Email everyone you know that might like to hear more about your P/S and ask them to sign up.

Getting the Most out of Your CRM

Use it as much as you can and keep it up to date. Most

CRMs also have an APP that you can download to your phone so you can use it anywhere. So download that!

Look at a typical day planned for you (or your sales or business development professional) when you open your CRM first thing in the morning.

Let's say you need to call Carla from XYZ Company today to finalize a sale (you can see the last email and communication you had with her) and then you need to send out a welcome email newsletter to a group of new sign-ups. You also need to answer a support call (you already know the history of the call because it's right in front of you on the customer's contact page) and then you have to follow up with a call about a sale with another contact.

The benefits of a CRM are many. When you have employees and you add them as users, you will see their daily activities. If you don't have employees yet, it will help you keep track of your sales pipeline. And although it may seem hard to set up – it's really not and the time you put into your CRM will pay off two-fold for you in sales and better customer service.

CHAPTER 11

Now go forth and make money!

You know, your P/S doesn't always have to be the best or the greatest or the least expensive. But it does have to be in the front of the mind of your customer so you have to be in front of that customer. That's much of the game of selling.

Here are some additional ideas for developing successful relationships for your business:

- Once you get up and running, treat your top ten customers to something – lunch, gift card, day at the spa, a promotion – it's easier to keep a great existing customer than to get a new customer.
- Send a survey out to your email list asking for feedback. Attach a motivation for the completion of the survey like a $25 gift card raffle, etc. I've used Survey Monkey for this in the past.
- Change your website content frequently.
- Remember that any business is a long-term commitment.

Great relationships take time to build.

• Use a written eBook or article about your P/S to add to your authority. Just ten thousand words can get you a ton of exposure!

• Always carry your business cards with you (with a small handful of tacks) and hand them out or pin them to business card bulletin boards.

• After a sale, send a branded handwritten thank you note.

• If you are a stay-at-home mom/dad starting a business, hold an open house (or a virtual open house on FaceBook Live), and showcase your P/S with snacks, coffee, and good conversation.

• Sign up for a Google business account and claim your business. It's free!!!

• If you have a brick and mortar store, see if there is anyone in town that you can partner with - like a complementary business - and see if you can leave a brochure/newsletter/business card on their counter and they can leave something on yours. When you partner with another business that is enthusiastic about your P/S, it can be a very beneficial relationship.

• Have fun. This is going to be an adventure, remember?

• Remember your determination and grit. That's the thing that's going to get you through. Just keep going and believe in yourself and your amazing P/S. And don't think, just do!

APPENDIX A: RESOURCES FOR STARTING A BUSINESS FROM THE SMALL BUSINESS ADMINISTRATION

The Small Business Administration is a great resource for any small business related topic. I encourage you to scour their website to get the latest information for helping your small business succeed. Http://www.SBA.Gov

How to write a business plan: https://www.sba.gov/business-guide/plan-your-business/write-your-business-plan

How to choose and claim your business name: https://www.sba.gov/blogs/how-choose-claim-and-protect-your-business-name-online-and-offline

Register your business: https://www.sba.gov/blogs/how-register-your-small-business-four-steps

Sole Proprietorship or LLC? Tips for choosing your business structure: https://www.sba.gov/business-guide/launch-your-business/choose-business-structure

What the deal with taxes on your small business?

https://www.sba.gov/business-guide/manage-your-business/pay-taxes?utm_medium=email&utm_source=govdelivery

How to patent your product: https://www.uspto.gov/patents-getting-started/general-information-concerning-patents

APPENDIX B: BUSINESS DEVELOPMENT OVERVIEW: STRATEGY BASED AROUND A PRODUCT

THE PLATE LIGHTER

One minute elevator pitch: A portable, solar and optional battery-powered ceramic plate heater with an adjustable light that clamps onto a plate and prevents your home/outdoor cooked meal from getting cold while you are:

- Waiting for everyone to come to the table
- Camping
- Waiting for other food to finish cooking
- Just sitting and eating
- Waiting for the power to come back on

Competitors:

- Portable plate warmers
- Nothing similar on the market

Domain name:

- Platelighter.com

Price point: $12.99

Distribution channel:

- Present:
  - Website
  - Small, local tradeshows
- Future:
  - Large camping retailers
  - Large home retailers
  - Investigate Amazon and Ebay

Marketing Strategy:

The problem that the Plate Lighter solves is it prevents you having to eat cold food when you are camping (or the fire goes out, or you're waiting for your family to come home/arrive at table)

Features:

- 2 light selections:
  - Firelight
  - Straight LED
- Warms the plate but never burns your hand
- Safe to the touch
- Long lasting charge from solar or rechargeable battery

- Ceramic heater never overcooks food

Benefits:

- Always serve hot food to your family
- Never lose all that hard work of cooking dinner
- Environmentally friendly
- Gives you the freedom of cooking good home made meals even while camping and RV'ing
- See your food even if the power goes out
- Easy on the eyes with two light settings
- Slow eater? Keeps your food warm even if you are on the "Get up from the table" diet

Basic messaging:

- Do you home cook only to have your food get cold while waiting for your family to come to the table?
- For just $12.99 you get four plate warmers that keep your food like it just came out of the oven.
- You'll never burn your hands with our patented ceramic heat source. Even if a child grabs it, it will never burn any skin.
- Easy to remove – slides right off your plate and can even go in the dishwasher!
- Great for camping with a light on your food (even if your power goes out, you'll always be able see what you are eating).

Marketing communications implementation:

- Design Logo in MS Word (It can be done!) or online designer (Canva)
- Design and order business cards on Vista print

Brochure:

Designed at home with printer and your own pictures (or stock photos from the web) of:

- Camping
- Eating your great home cooked meal with friends
- Happy people eating
- The product itself and an illustration of how it works
- Include benefits to the customer
- Brochure to be left at campsites (leave a few of the Plate Lighters with the campground managers)
- Create content including videos and images

Website:

- After signing up for hosting and domain name, use an easy Wordpress template to design website – or have Hosting company design e-commerce site.
- Include blog with recipes
    - Create blog plan with content
- Sign up for Paypal to accept payments

AND/OR

- Develop Plate Lighter Social Media presence
    - Create Facebook page to be your website
    - Create posts that act like a blog
    - Create a group about camping recipes
    - Create Twitter account - @platelighter
    - Tweet your recipes, product usage ideas, product updates, images of customers, or product benefits
- Create a Podcast about cooking while camping

Email newsletter:

- Sign up for Constant Contact or MailChimp
- Reach out to all friends/colleagues on Facebook, email, text, Twitter, Linkedin and request they sign up!
- Send one newsletter a month filled with recipes, product images, and ways to use the Plate Lighter.

Tradeshows:

Research local tradeshows for the following information:

- Be where campers are
- Boy Scout conferences?
- 4h fairs/Boat Shows
- Visit RV shows and talk to RV manufacturers about having Plate Lighter packaged with RVs
- Visit/call those tradeshows and research the different attendee

Notes:

Notes:

Notes:

Notes:

Notes:

Notes:

ABOUT THE AUTHOR

L.A. Dyer has been in corporate communications for over 30 years writing and designing for both Fortune 500 companies as well as small and start-up organizations. Visit http://www.LADyerbooks.com for more exciting products from this author.

www.ingramcontent.com/pod-product-compliance
Lightning Source LLC
Chambersburg PA
CBHW071055240526
45469CB00006BD/2302